WINTER WHITE

Joanne Ryder

Illustrated by Carol Lacey

Morrow Junior Books
NEW YORK

Author's Note

This story was inspired by a trip I took to the Far North, where winter is long and dark and there is sometimes more snow than you can imagine.

Like Fox and Lemming, real arctic foxes and collared lemmings have coats of dark fur in summer that change to white in the winter so they blend into their snow-covered world.

Acrylic paints on vellum bristol board were used for the full-color illustrations.
The text type is 15-point Giovanni.

Text copyright © 1997 by Joanne Ryder
Illustrations copyright © 1997 by Carol Lacey

Printed in Hong Kong by South China Printing Company (1988) Ltd.

1 2 3 4 5 6 7 8 9 10

Library of Congress Cataloging-in-Publication Data
Ryder, Joanne.
Winter white/Joanne Ryder; illustrated by Carol Lacey.
p. cm.
Summary: Because they never give up hope and always want
to change the present into something better, Fox and Lemming
annually trick Winter into trading snow for sun.
ISBN 0-688-12992-7 (trade)—ISBN 0-688-12993-5 (library)
[1. Winter—Fiction.   2. Foxes—Fiction.   3. Lemmings—Fiction.]
I. Lacey, Carol, ill.   II. Title.   PZ7.R959Wi 1996   [E]—dc20   95-35387   CIP AC

For Kathy Yep, who danced for joy in the snow, with love
—J.R.

To Brendan and Annalisa
—C.L.

If you ever meet Fox or Lemming, be careful. Tricksters by nature, they are always ready to take a chance or make a trade, hoping they can change *now* for something better.

And between schemes, the two will bet on anything for fun.

"Just to keep in practice," chirps Lemming with a nimble leap.

"For the pleasure of the game," sweetly barks Fox with a wave of his graceful tail.

So one hot day a long time ago, Fox bet Lemming that the next mosquito would bite her first. But Fox lost the bet.

The next mosquito bit a newcomer climbing up their rocky hill. And though it was the brightest of days at the top of the world, watchful Lemming saw that the stranger left no shadow.

"This might be interesting," she whispered to Fox.

Furry and white, the newcomer looked like a huge bear to her. Fox wasn't as sure. But when the stranger yelped, they saw inside his wide mouth. It was dark, very dark.

"Mosquitoes a bit pesky around here," said the stranger, scratching his freshly bitten paw.

"No more than usual, dear sir," said Fox as he flicked a hundred hungry insects away from his nose.

"I know something that will chase them off," said the stranger.

He opened his wide dark mouth, and tiny Lemming drew back, wondering whether he was going to roar and frighten the dark cloud of mosquitoes that circled around him or even swallow it whole!

Instead, the stranger sang a high howling tune. From the sky, tiny bits of whiteness, bright like stars, began to fall. They landed gently and covered everything and everyone in a soft, cool blanket. The mosquitoes, chilled and confused, swirled off and out of sight.

"What marvel is this?" asked Fox, sniffing a pile of this new thing and smelling nothing.

"I call it…snow," declared the stranger.

If we could trade for something that will chase mosquitoes away, thought Lemming, everybody in the world will be happier.

"How grand this snow looks and feels," sighed Fox, and he danced in circles, leaving pretty tracks behind him. As Lemming danced with him under the bright sun, their paws felt light and cool.

Lemming dug tunnels in the snow, and Fox couldn't find her. They played hide-and-seek, and Lemming won more than she lost.

"I like this snow," she said. "Small animals will feel safe in it."

"Would you consider a trade, dear sir?" Fox asked. "We have whatever you see here—rocks, sea, sun.… Name it, and it is yours."

"Hmmm," said the stranger. "I could use the sun."

"A good trade," Lemming whispered to Fox. "We have lots of sun."

"A splendid deal," said Fox. "I'm certain the other animals would agree if they were here."

"But," said Lemming, gazing high and meeting the stranger's eyes, "we'd want a lot of snow for the sun."

"You'll have more than you can imagine," said the stranger, standing so tall he blocked the sun from Lemming's view. "Though it may take even me some time. What if I take a little bit of sun each day and bring you lots of snow later?"

"No tricks," said Lemming.

"You have my word," said the stranger, shaking their paws and smiling.

"What is your word without your name?" asked Fox.

And as he ran down the rocky hill, the stranger called back, "My name? It's Winter."

At first no one noticed that the days were shorter. A little more sun disappeared each day. Soon, though, it was dark much of the time. All that darkness made the animals very sleepy. They slept more and more in the cool, dark night.

In the darkness, Fox and Lemming began to worry that they had been cheated. But one morning Winter returned.

"Where is our snow?" they shouted at him. "We want it now!"

"Here," howled Winter. "Here and here and here it is."

As the sparkling snow fell, Lemming and Fox rolled in its coolness till it covered them.

"Oh, my friend, look at you," said Fox, laughing at the white Lemming.

"Look at yourself," said Lemming.

They both tried to shake the bright snow off, but they couldn't shake its whiteness. Their fur was no longer dark but snow-white.

"You wanted snow," said Winter, chuckling at their confusion. "I thought everyone should see whom to thank for this wonderful trade."

Each day Winter brought more and more snow, and took a bit more sun. As Fox had imagined, the snow chased the mosquitoes away. But it also chilled the animals to their bones, and the freezing nights killed the plants and grass the animals ate.

"Who did this terrible thing to us?" asked graceful Caribou.

"Who stole our sun?" asked tiny Redpoll.

"Ask those two," snorted Walrus. "Ask the fools who are white as the snow."

"It was that rascal Winter," said Fox.

"He tricked us," said Lemming.

So everyone knew whom to blame. Winter—and Fox and Lemming, who traded the sun away without asking anyone.

"Snow for the sun," the animals cried. "What fools!"

The other animals tried to think how to get the sun back, but no one could. So they gave up ever seeing its cheery brightness and feeling its warmth again. Some dug tunnels in the soft snow and fell asleep. The sleek ones, with flippers and fins, slid under the ice-covered seas to hunt in the waters, now cold and dark.

Only Fox and Lemming stayed to plan.

"There is always a way," said Lemming. "You just dig deeper, talk faster, think harder. There is always a way."

"Indeed," said Fox, his tail high. "And we are the ones who will find it."

With the sun gone, the moon wandered alone across a dark sky. Over the vast moonlit plains of snow and ice, Fox and Lemming hunted Winter.

Blizzards blew around them till they could barely see each other. With legs cold and stiff as sticks, the two animals crept ever onward.

"Winter is that way," said Fox, sniffing the air with his fine nose. "I smell his bitter scent."

Winter hid in his cave deep in the snow.

Lemming said, "I bet I can find him."

She dug with her small fine claws and paws, deeper and deeper, looking this way and that.

"I see something bright," called Lemming.

"Be wary," said Fox, following her as she dug to the mouth of Winter's cave. "I smell someone sneaky coming."

It was Winter. He saw the two huddled before him and laughed with a yawn and a shake of his big paws, claws spread wide.

Winter howled and blew a blinding blast of snow and wind to chase them away from the mouth of his bright cave. Fox and Lemming were almost frozen with cold and fear, but they would not run away.

"Why are you here?" Winter roared. "To make another trade?"

"Yes," shouted the two animals.

"What do you fools have that I could want?" Winter asked.

Then Fox and Lemming offered Winter all they had and all they knew.

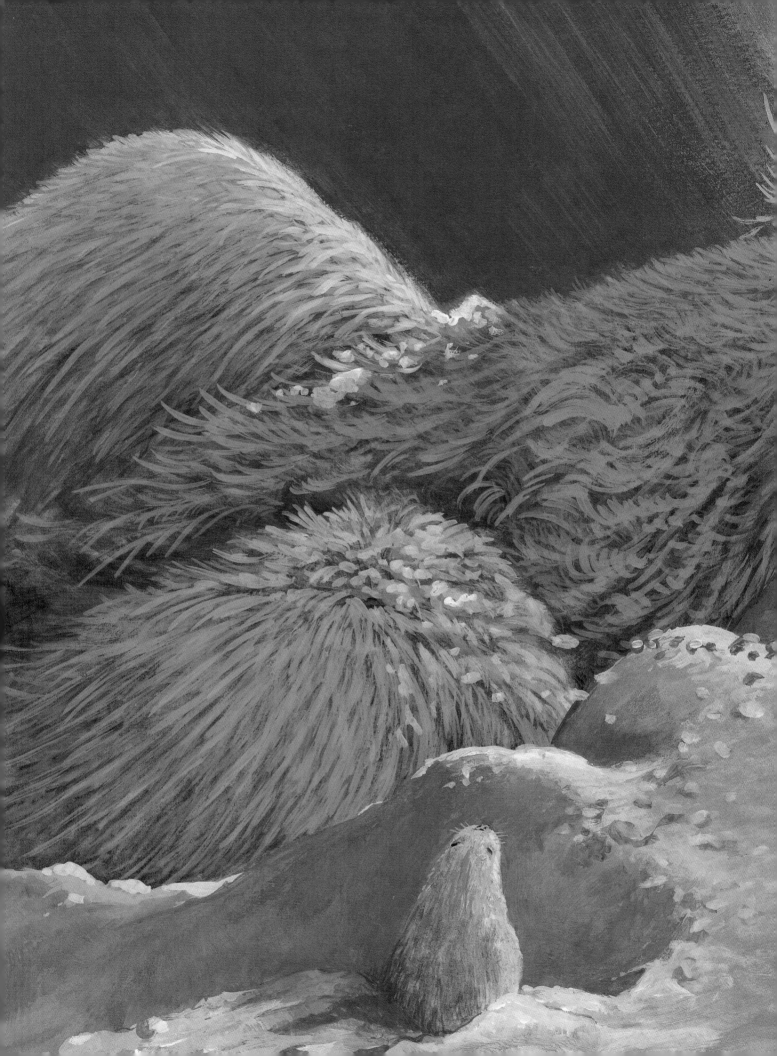

"I know where golden rocks glow in the earth," said
Lemming. "You can have all the gold you wish."

"I have the sun," said Winter, yawning grandly. "No rock
can glow like the sun."

"Someone so grand should not hunt for his food," said
Fox. "With my keen nose, I will hunt for you, Winter. You will
never be hungry again."

"With my great jaws and sharp claws, I can always catch
food," said Winter with a bigger yawn.

On and on Fox and Lemming went, trying to find
something to trade for the sun. But all they had and all they
knew were not enough to change Winter's mind.

"That's it," groaned Fox. "It's over."

A weary Winter nodded and stretched his mouth in the
biggest yawn yet, till his wide jaws cracked.

Ever watchful, Lemming got an idea. "You look so tired,
Winter," she said. "Aren't you getting enough sleep?"

"Not really," said Winter. "I don't sleep well in my cave anymore."

Fox quickly grasped Lemming's plan.

"Ah, that sun is brilliant and blinding," he said. "Everyone here sleeps so much deeper in the darkness now."

"Darkness brings us such sweet dreams," said Lemming. "Long nights make for the best rest."

"Really," said Winter, rubbing his sleepy eyes. "I do miss the dark sometimes.

"Maybe…," he said, pausing to stare at the faint glow that flickered from the mouth of his cave. Fox and Lemming did not move, did not breathe, until Winter said, "Maybe I have too much sun. Perhaps I could trade for some darkness."

So Winter sang a deep song of the earth. The warm song began to melt the snow and call the sun. Humming sleepily, Winter went off to get some rest.

Fox and Lemming watched the distant sky and waited for the sun to creep out of Winter's cave. And when the edge of the sky turned pink and then gold, the two animals, winter white, danced in the brightness of morning come again.

The next day the sun stayed longer, so Winter could nap a little more. And the day after that the sun stayed longer still. Soon it was light more than it was dark, and everyone woke up and danced with Fox and Lemming.

You might think those two would learn, but every year it's the same. Winter gets tired of sleeping and tricks them into trading for the sun. Each year, when the sunless world is bleak, Fox and Lemming find a way to trick him into trading back. Because they never give up hope, they once more change *now* into something better. When they do, the days grow longer again....

Some say the pair are just too foolish to be believed. But if you go out on a midwinter night, you will see the two of them, white as snow, dancing in the moonlight. They dance with delight, knowing the sun will shine again.

To win back a treasure lost brings joy, and such joy is rare, even for the wise.